T0327878

2ND EDITION

Activity Book 2A

Sweet factory numbers

Date: _____

Know the value of each digit in a 2-digit number up to 50

You will need:
• coloured pencils

Teacher's notes

Children look at the numbers on the jars and draw a line to match two sweets to the jars to which they belong. Then they colour each pair of sweets to match the jars.

paceships and stars

ompare numbers up to 50, using the reater than (>) and less than (<) signs

Date: _____

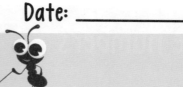

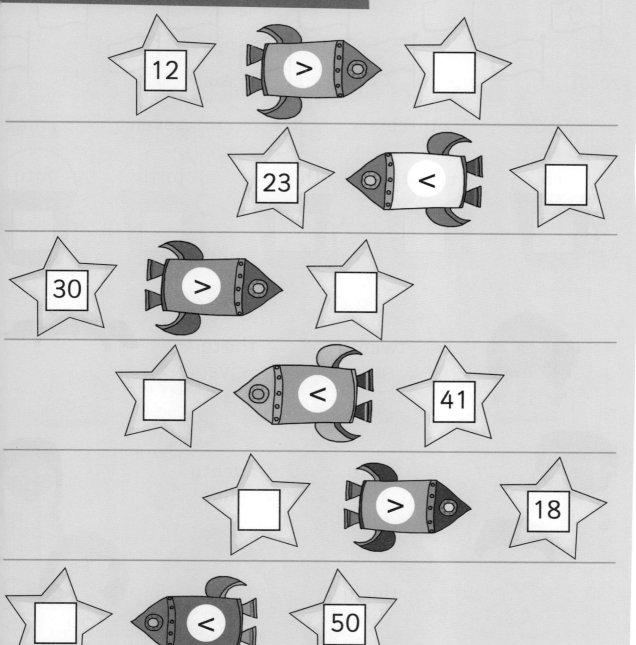

Children look at the number and the inequality sign in each row and then write a number that is greater than or less than the number shown.

Date: _____

Seaside numbers

Read and write numbers to 50

You will need:
• coloured pencils

0

zero   two   four   six   eight

one   three   five   seven   nine

ten   twenty   thirty   forty   fifty

33

21

42

twenty
-one

forty
-two

thirty
-three

thirty
-five

twenty
-nine

forty
-eight

48

35

29

Teacher's notes

At the top of the page, children look at the numbers written in words on the sandcastles and above the buckets and write the numbers in numerals into the spaces on the flags and buckets. At the bottom of the page, children draw lines to match each child to the swim ring showing the same number in words as the numeral on their T-shirt.

4

10s and 1s trees

Solve problems about place value

Date: _____

You will need:
- four counters
- coloured pencils

	tens +		ones =	
	tens +		ones =	
	tens +		ones =	
	tens +		ones =	
	tens +		ones =	

Teacher's notes

Children explore the numbers that they can make by drawing four apples on each pair of tens and ones trees in different combinations. They should use four counters to support their investigation before drawing the apples on to the trees.

Date: _____

Add both ways

Add two numbers in any order

| 5 | + | | = | |
| 7 | + | | = | |

| | + | | = | |
| | + | | = | |

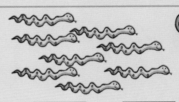

| | + | | = | |
| | + | | = | |

| | + | | = | |
| | + | | = | |

| | + | | = | |
| | + | | = | |

| | + | | = | |
| | + | | = | |

Teacher's notes

Children complete the two matching addition facts for each set of pictures.

Date: _____

Cloudy calculations

Recall and use addition and subtraction facts to 20

3 + 6 = ☐

7 + 5 = ☐

4 + 9 = ☐

13 + 4 = ☐

2 + 16 = ☐

12 + 7 = ☐

9 – 5 = ☐

7 – 5 = ☐

10 – 7 = ☐

14 – 14 = ☐

11 – 8 = ☐

15 – 6 = ☐

12 plus 6 ☐

7 more than 8 ☐

18 take away 5 ☐

Subtract 8 from 13 ☐

Teacher's notes

Children complete the calculations and number sentences, writing the answers as numerals.
If needed interlocking cubes can be used to help children.

Checking fish facts

- Use addition to check the answer to subtraction
- Use subtraction to check the answer to addition

| 7 | + | | = | |
| 12 | – | | = | |

| | + | | = | |
| | – | | = | |

| | – | | = | |
| | + | | = | |

| | – | | = | |
| | + | | = | |

Teacher's notes

At the top of the page, children write an addition calculation about the fish and then check their answer, using a subtraction calculation. At the bottom of the page, they write a subtraction calculation about the fish and then check their answer, using an addition calculation.

Date: _____

'Take away' or 'difference'

nderstand subtraction as both
ake away' and 'difference'

$18 - 12 =$ | 6

+ 6

0 1 2 3 4 5 6 7 8 9 10 11 (12) 13 14 15 16 17 (18) 19 20

$17 - 4 =$ | 13

− 4

0 1 2 3 4 5 6 7 8 9 10 11 12 (13) 14 15 16 (17) 18 19 20

$11 - 2 =$

0 1 2 3 4 5 6 7 8 9 10 11 12 13 14 15 16 17 18 19 20

$13 - 9 =$

0 1 2 3 4 5 6 7 8 9 10 11 12 13 14 15 16 17 18 19 20

$19 - 14 =$

0 1 2 3 4 5 6 7 8 9 10 11 12 13 14 15 16 17 18 19 20

$16 - 5 =$

0 1 2 3 4 5 6 7 8 9 10 11 12 13 14 15 16 17 18 19 20

$12 - 6 =$

0 1 2 3 4 5 6 7 8 9 10 11 12 13 14 15 16 17 18 19 20

Teacher's notes

Children decide whether it is better to subtract (take away) one number from the other or find the difference between each pair of numbers. The first example shows difference, the second take away. They draw on the number line and then complete the calculation.

9

Date: _____

Name that shape

Name 2-D shapes

| pentagon | hexagon | octagon | triangle |

sides: ⬜

vertices: ⬜

name: _____

sides: ⬜

vertices: ⬜

name: _____

sides: ⬜

vertices: ⬜

sides: ⬜

vertices: ⬜

name: _____

sides: ⬜

vertices: ⬜

name: _____

sides: ⬜

vertices: ⬜

sides: ⬜

vertices: ⬜

name: _____

sides: ⬜

vertices: ⬜

name: _____

sides: ⬜

vertices: ⬜

Teacher's notes

Children count the number of sides and vertices of each 2-D shape, filling in the answer boxes, and write its name, using the shape names at the top of the page. Remind children that 'vertices' means 'corners'.

10

Which shapes have symmetry?

nd shapes with a vertical line of symmetry

Date: _____

You will need:
- mirror
- ruler
- coloured pencils

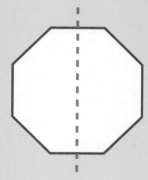

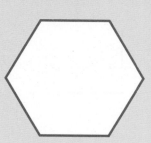

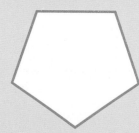

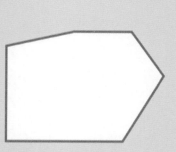

Teacher's notes

Children guess the line of symmetry then place a mirror on each shape along their predicted line of symmetry to see if they are correct. They draw the line of symmetry with a ruler and colour the shapes that are symmetrical. Then they write the name of each shape underneath.

Date: _____

Drawing shapes

Draw common 2-D shapes with a ruler

You will need:
- ruler

Complete these squares.

Complete these rectangles.

Complete these triangles.

Teacher's notes

Children use a ruler to complete the squares, rectangles and triangles. Then they use the space to draw their own square, rectangle and triangle.

12

Date: _____

ort it out!

ort shapes by comparing them

You will need:
• Resource 2:
  2-D shape cards

circle   oval   triangle   square   rectangle
pentagon   hexagon   octagon

Fewer than 4 vertices	4 vertices	More than 4 vertices
circle		

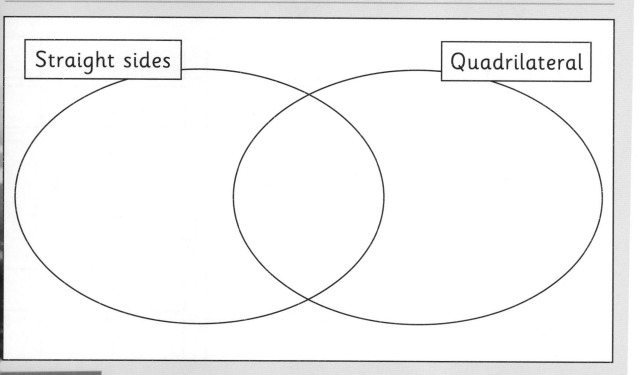

Straight sides

Quadrilateral

Teacher's notes

Children write each shape name in the correct section of the sorting diagram and then in the Venn diagram. Remind children that some shapes may belong outside the interlocking rings.

Number flowers

Date: _____

Recall and use addition and subtraction facts to 20

| 15 | + | 3 | = | 18 |

| 15 | − | 3 | = | 12 |

☐ + ☐ = ☐

☐ − ☐ = ☐

☐ + ☐ = ☐

☐ − ☐ = ☐

☐ + ☐ = ☐

☐ − ☐ = ☐

☐ + ☐ = ☐

☐ − ☐ = ☐

☐ + ☐ = ☐

☐ − ☐ = ☐

☐ + ☐ = ☐

☐ − ☐ = ☐

☐ + ☐ = ☐

☐ − ☐ = ☐

☐ + ☐ = ☐

☐ − ☐ = ☐

Teacher's notes

Children use each pair of numbers on the flowers to create one addition and one subtraction calculation. Remind children that they should put the larger number first in each calculation.

Date: _____

elated addition facts

se related facts to answer questions

30 + 10 = ☐

3 + 1 = ☐

40 + 10 = ☐

☐ + ☐ = ☐

60 + 20 = ☐

☐ + ☐ = ☐

50 + 40 = ☐

☐ + ☐ = ☐

70 + 30 = ☐

☐ + ☐ = ☐

80 + 10 = ☐

☐ + ☐ = ☐

20 + 30 = ☐

3 + 2 = ☐

10 + 50 = ☐

☐ + ☐ = ☐

30 + 40 = ☐

☐ + ☐ = ☐

10 + 70 = ☐

☐ + ☐ = ☐

40 + 60 = ☐

☐ + ☐ = ☐

20 + 50 = ☐

☐ + ☐ = ☐

Teacher's notes

Children write the related addition calculation using one-digit numbers that helps them solve each given addition calculation involving multiples of 10. For the second half of the page, remind children that putting the larger number first makes addition quicker.

15

Related subtraction facts

Date: _____

Use related facts to answer questions

40 – 20 = ☐

4 – 2 = ☐

30 – 10 = ☐

☐ – ☐ = ☐

60 – 40 = ☐

☐ – ☐ = ☐

70 – 30 = ☐

☐ – ☐ = ☐

50 – 20 = ☐

☐ – ☐ = ☐

90 – 30 = ☐

☐ – ☐ = ☐

80 – 50 = ☐

☐ – ☐ = ☐

70 – 40 = ☐

☐ – ☐ = ☐

100 – 60 = ☐

☐ – ☐ = ☐

90 – 70 = ☐

☐ – ☐ = ☐

60 – 30 = ☐

☐ – ☐ = ☐

50 – 40 = ☐

☐ – ☐ = ☐

Teacher's notes

Children write the related subtraction calculation using one-digit numbers that helps them solve each given subtraction calculation involving multiples of 10.

Date: _____

Calculation patterns

Use patterns of similar calculations

11 + 0 = 11

10 + ☐ = 11

☐ + 2 = 11

8 + 3 = ☐

☐ + ☐ = 11

6 + 5 = ☐

5 + ☐ = ☐

☐ + 7 = 11

☐ + ☐ = ☐

2 + ☐ = 11

☐ + 10 = ☐

☐ + ☐ = ☐

11 − 0 = 11

☐ − 1 = 10

11 − 2 = ☐

11 − ☐ = 8

☐ − 4 = ☐

11 − ☐ = 6

☐ − ☐ = 5

11 − ☐ = ☐

☐ − ☐ = ☐

11 − 9 = ☐

11 − ☐ = 1

☐ − ☐ = ☐

9 + 3 = 12   ☐ + 2 = 12   15 + 4 = 19   14 + ☐ = 19

Teacher's notes

At the top of the page, children complete the number facts for 11. At the bottom of the page, they answer questions using related given facts.

17

Date: _____

Cake addition

Add 1s to a multiple of 10

You will need:
- Resource 4: 1–100 number square (optional)

20 + 6 =

40 + 3 =

10 + 9 =

50 + 7 =

30 + 5 =

60 + 2 =

80 + 1 =

70 + 8 =

90 + 4 =

30 + 2 =

60 + 7 =

20 + 5 =

90 + 6 =

40 + 9 =

80 + 8 =

Teacher's notes

Children work out the answers to the addition calculations. They can use a 1–100 number square for support, if needed.

Date: _____

at subtraction

ubtract 1s from a multiple of 10

You will need:
- Resource 4:
  1–100 number
  square (optional)

10 – 3 = ☐

40 – 5 = ☐

20 – 9 = ☐

30 – 8 = ☐

60 – 1 = ☐

50 – 7 = ☐

80 – 4 = ☐

70 – 6 = ☐

90 – 2 = ☐

20 – 4 = ☐

50 – 2 = ☐

40 – 6 = ☐

90 – 5 = ☐

60 – 9 = ☐

80 – 3 = ☐

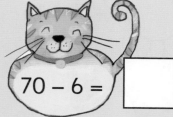

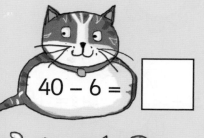

Teacher's notes

Children work out the answers to the subtraction calculations. They can use a 1–100 number square for support, if needed.

Date: _____

Missing number flowers

Solve missing number problems involving addition

5 + ⬭ = 9

⬭ + 7 = 12

8 + ⬭ = 15

⬭ + 6 = 11

8 + ⬭ = 14

⬭ + 9 = 17

4 + ⬭ = 13

⬭ + 7 = 16

5 + ⬭ = 12

⬭ + 4 = 17

5 + ⬭ = 18

⬭ + 2 = 14

3 + ⬭ = 15

⬭ + 2 = 17

6 + ⬭ = 19

⬭ + 15 = 19

11 + ⬭ = 16

⬭ + 12 = 18

Teacher's notes

Children solve the missing number addition calculations and write the missing numbers on the flowers.

Missing number bubbles

Date: _____

Solve missing number problems involving subtraction

$8 - \boxed{} = 2$

$\boxed{} - 4 = 3$

$7 - \boxed{} = 5$

$\boxed{} - 5 = 12$

$14 - \boxed{} = 11$

$\boxed{} - 6 = 13$

$18 - \boxed{} = 15$

$\boxed{} - 7 = 10$

$15 - \boxed{} = 12$

$\boxed{} - 4 = 11$

$19 - \boxed{} = 14$

$\boxed{} - 2 = 14$

$18 - \boxed{} = 5$

$\boxed{} - 16 = 2$

$17 - \boxed{} = 3$

$\boxed{} - 15 = 1$

$19 - \boxed{} = 5$

$\boxed{} - 12 = 6$

Teacher's notes

Children solve the missing number subtraction calculations and write the missing numbers on the bubbles.

All about length

Estimate and measure lengths

Date: _____

You will need:
• ruler

litres	centimetres	grams	metres	kilograms

My estimate: ☐ cm   Actual: ☐ cm

My estimate: ☐ cm   Actual: ☐ cm

My estimate: ☐ cm   Actual: ☐ cm

My estimate: ☐ cm   Actual: ☐ cm

Teacher's notes

At the top of the page, children circle the pictures of the equipment, and then the units, used to measure length. At the bottom of the page, they estimate the length of each piece of string in the pictures and then measure them.

Date: _____

Heights and widths

Choose units to measure height and length

centimetres   metres

centimetres   metres

centimetres   metres

centimetres   metres

centimetres   metres

centimetres   metres

centimetres   metres

centimetres   metres

centimetres   metres

centimetres	metres

Teacher's notes

At the top of the page, children decide whether the objects in the pictures would be measured in centimetres or metres and circle the appropriate word. At the bottom of the page, children write or draw other objects that would be measured in either centimetres or metres.

23

Date: _____

Recording lengths using the signs >, < or =

Measure and compare lengths, using >, < or =

You will need:
• ruler

A _____ ☐ cm
B _____ ☐ cm
C _____ ☐ cm
D _____ ☐ cm
E _____ ☐ cm
F _____ ☐ cm
G _____ ☐ cm
H _____ ☐ cm

shortest   longest

☐ ☐ ☐ ☐ ☐ ☐ ☐ ☐

8 cm >	2 cm	12 cm =	8 cm + 4 cm
5 cm <		11 cm =	
12 cm >		2 cm =	
11 cm <		7 cm =	
2 cm <		4 cm =	
7 cm >		8 cm =	

Teacher's notes

Children measure each line and write its length in the space provided. They order the lines, shortest to longest. Children then use the lengths measured to complete each number statement, for example, 8 cm > 2 cm. They complete the equals number statements by adding and/or subtracting pairs of different lengths, for example, 12 cm = 8 cm + 4 cm. Encourage them to find different possibilities.

Date: _____

alf as long

easure and compare lengths

You will need:
• ruler

☐ cm

☐ cm

☐ cm

☐ cm

☐ cm

☐ cm

Teacher's notes

Children measure the length of each line and write it beside the line. Then they draw a line that is half the length underneath each one and label this length. Encourage children to check their lengths by doubling the shorter line to see if this equals the longer line.

25

Stepping stones of 2

Date: _____

Count in steps of 2

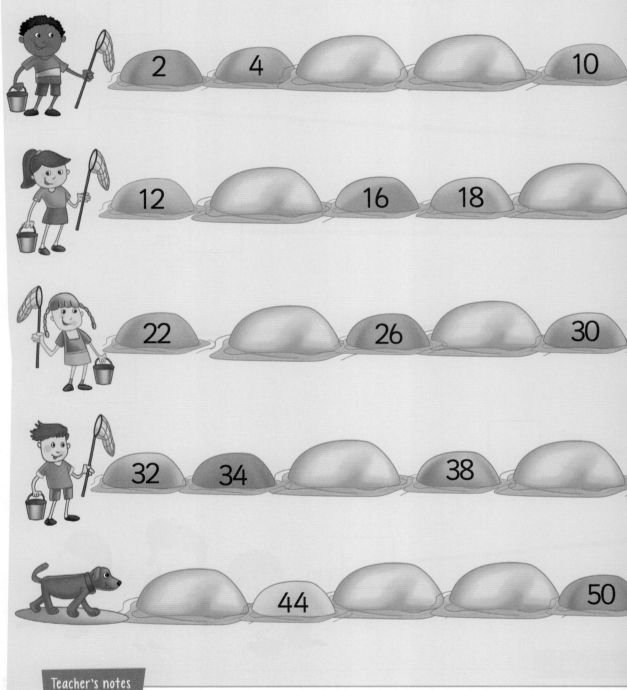

Row 1: 2, 4, __, __, 10

Row 2: 12, __, 16, 18, __

Row 3: 22, __, 26, __, 30

Row 4: 32, 34, __, 38, __

Row 5: __, 44, __, __, 50

Teacher's notes

Children look at each row of stepping stones and continue to count on in twos. They write the missing multiples of 2 into each space provided.

26

Date: _____

Birthday 2s

Understand the multiplication facts for the 2 multiplication table

You will need:
• coloured pencils

☐ candles

3 × 2

2 × 2

☐ candles

☐ candles

1 × 2

☐ candles

4 × 2

8 × 2

☐ candles

6 × 2

☐ candles

7 × 2

5 × 2

☐ candles

☐ candles

Teacher's notes

Children look at each plate and write the number of candles in the space provided. Then they draw a line to the party hat showing the correct calculation and colour the plate to match.

27

Space division

Date: _____

Understand the division facts for the 2 multiplication table

You will need:
• two coloured pencils

$6 \div 2$

$4 \div 2$

$2 \div 2$

$8 \div 2$

$16 \div 2$

$12 \div 2$

$14 \div 2$

$10 \div 2$

Teacher's notes

For each planet, children share the rocks equally between the two astronauts. They use two colours to show how many rocks each astronaut gets. Then they draw a line to join each planet with the star showing the matching calculation.

Date: _____

Sweet shop solutions

Solve problems involving multiplication and division

You will need:
• counters

Mr Cole has 8 jars of sweets to fit evenly on 2 shelves. How many jars will he put on each shelf?

☐ ÷ ☐ = ☐

Cavan and Theo both buy a bag of sweets. There are 3 sweets in each bag. How many sweets altogether?

☐ × ☐ = ☐

Lucy takes her 2 brothers to the shop. She buys each of them 2 lollipops. How many lollies does Lucy buy?

☐ × ☐ = ☐

Mr Cole has 10 packets of stickers. Half of them are dinosaur stickers and half are car stickers. How many packs are there of each sticker?

☐ ÷ ☐ = ☐

Mr Cole has 12 chocolate eggs. He gives 2 eggs to each child. How many children are given chocolates?

☐ ÷ ☐ = ☐

Caie, Jasmine, Meena and Bo all buy 2 packets of crisps each. How many packets do they buy altogether?

☐ × ☐ = ☐

Teacher's notes

Children read each word problem carefully, then write the multiplication or division calculation in the spaces provided. They can use counters to help work out the answers, if needed.

Submarine sequences of 5

Date: _____

Count in steps of 5

5   10   ○   20   ○

20   ○   30   ○   40

45   ○   55   60   ○

65   70   ○   80   ○

80   ○   ○   95   100

Teacher's notes

Children look at each row of fish and submarines. They continue to count on in fives and write the missing multiples of 5 onto each submarine.

Date: _____

lower 5s

nderstand the multiplication facts for the 5 multiplication table

0   5   10   15   20   25   30   35   40   45   50

1 × 5   2 × 5   15

3 × 5   4 × 5   25   5

5 × 5   6 × 5   20

7 × 5   8 × 5   35   10

9 × 5   10 × 5   40   45

50   30

Teacher's notes

Children look at the multiplication fact on each flower and draw a line to match it to the bee showing the correct answer. They can use the number track at the top of the page to help them count in fives.

Chip sharing

Date: _____

Understand the division facts for the 5 multiplication table

☐ ÷ 5 = ☐

☐ ÷ 5 = ☐

☐ ÷ 5 = ☐

☐ ÷ 5 = ☐

☐ ÷ 5 = ☐

Teacher's notes

For each row of plates children count the total number of chips and complete the division calculation by writing the missing numbers in the boxes.

Date: _____

upermarket solutions

lve problems involving multiplication and division

You will need:
- counters

Aaron has 5 coins.
Each coin is a 5p coin.
How much does
Aaron have
to spend?

[ ] × [ ] = [ ]

Min buys 20 sweets.
She gives 5 sweets to each
of her friends.
How many
friends get
sweets?

[ ] ÷ [ ] = [ ]

Ella buys 40 strawberries.
She puts 5 strawberries
in each bag.
How many bags
of strawberries
does she have?

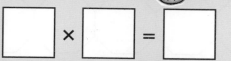

[ ] ÷ [ ] = [ ]

Ellis buys 4 packs
of pencils. Each
pack has 5 pencils
inside. How many
pencils are there
altogether?

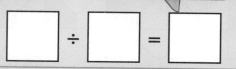

[ ] × [ ] = [ ]

Samir has 30 apples.
He shares them
equally between
5 bags. How many
apples in each bag?

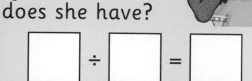

[ ] ÷ [ ] = [ ]

Holly buys 9 packs
of stickers. Each
pack has 5 stickers
inside. How many
stickers does she
have altogether?

[ ] × [ ] = [ ]

Teacher's notes

Children read each word problem carefully and then write the multiplication or division calculation in the spaces provided. Encourage them to use counters to help work out the answers, if needed.

Spot the pattern

Date: _____

Continue patterns and sequences, using 2-D shapes

You will need:
- coloured pencils
- ruler

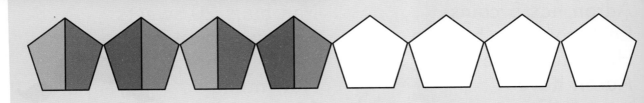

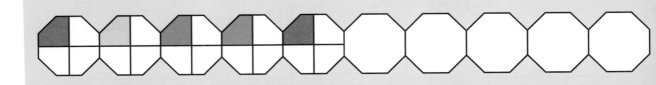

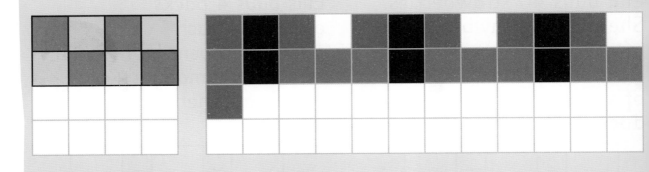

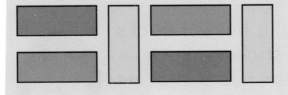

Teacher's notes

For the first three rows children look at the pattern and continue the sequence by drawing lines and colouring the shapes. For the last two rows children draw and colour the shapes to continue the sequence.

Date: _____

Creating shape patterns

create patterns and sequences

You will need:
- coloured pencils
- ruler

repeat	first	second	third

My pattern has _____.

My pattern has _____.

My pattern has _____.

My pattern has _____.

Teacher's notes

Children create 2-D shape patterns, using different grids as support. Then they describe each pattern, using mathematical language from the word bank, for example: My pattern has a blue square then a red square and it repeats.

35

Shape grid

Date: _____

Find the position of a square on a grid of squares

Purple octagon | A1

Blue hexagon | ⬚

Green circle | ⬚

Yellow triangle | ⬚

	A	B	C	D
4		●	⬠	
3	⯃	⬡		△
2	⬠			
1	⯃	▭	◻	

---

2 squares to the right of the purple octagon

is the _____.

3 squares to the left of the yellow triangle

is the _____.

3 squares above the pink rectangle

is the _____.

2 squares below the orange octagon

is the _____.

Teacher's notes

In the top section, children write which square the shape is in. In the bottom section, children complete the sentences.

X marks the spot

Date: _____

Follow directions, using north, south, east and west

- Start on A. Move 3 squares east. Move 1 square south.

- Start on B. Move 1 square south. Move 2 squares west.

- Start on C. Move 2 squares east. Move 2 squares south.

- Start on D. Move 2 squares north. Move 2 squares east. Move 1 square south. Move 3 squares west.

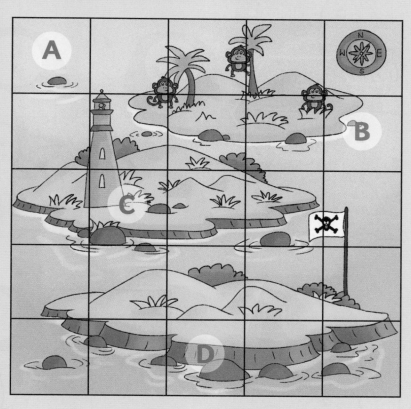

Start on A. _____ Finish on B.

Start on C. _____ Finish on D.

Start on D. _____ Finish on A.

Start on B. _____ Finish on D.

Teacher's notes

Children follow the directions and mark with an X where the treasure can be found, in all four places.
Then they write their own directions to take them between the points.

Date: _____

Tentacle 10s

Count in steps of 10

0			30
30		50	
	60		80
70			100

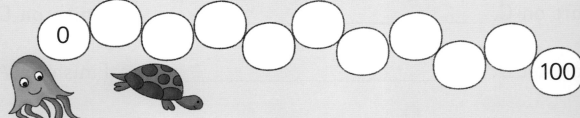

| 0 | | | | | | | | | | 100 |

Teacher's notes

Children complete each sequence by counting in tens and writing the correct numbers into the spaces on the rocks. Then, underneath, they complete the 0–100 number track, writing in all the missing multiples of 10.

Date: _____

Tomato 10s

Understand the multiplication facts for the 10 multiplication table

10 20 30 40 50 60 70 80 90 100

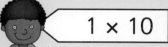 1 × 10

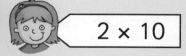 2 × 10

 3 × 10

 4 × 10

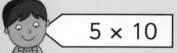 5 × 10

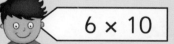 6 × 10

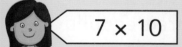 7 × 10

 8 × 10

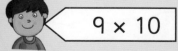 9 × 10

 10 × 10

 20

 70

 30

10

60

 50

 40

100

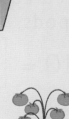 80

 90

Teacher's notes

Children draw a line to match each multiplication calculation to the tomato plant showing the correct answer.

Pea pod division

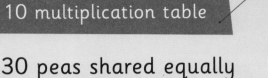

Understand the division facts for the 10 multiplication table

50 peas shared equally between 10 pods.

50 ÷ 10 = ☐

30 peas shared equally between 10 pods.

30 ÷ 10 = ☐

20 peas shared equally between 10 pods.

20 ÷ 10 = ☐

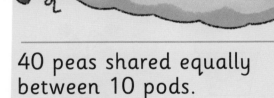

70 peas shared equally between 10 pods.

☐

70 ÷ 10 =

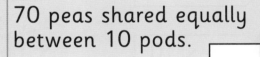
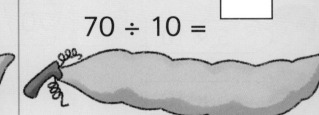

40 peas shared equally between 10 pods.

40 ÷ 10 = ☐

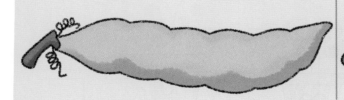

60 peas shared equally between 10 pods.

☐

60 ÷ 10 =

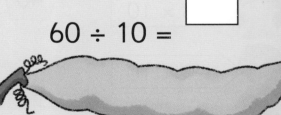

Teacher's notes

Children work out how many peas there will be in each pea pod when they are shared equally between 10 pods. They complete each division fact and draw the number of peas that will be in each pea pod.

Multiply or divide?

Date: _____

Solve problems involving multiplication and division

Malkeet buys 5 pens for 10p each. How much does he spend?

☐ ◯ ☐ ◯ ☐

20 children get into 10 dodgems. How many children are there in each one?

☐ ◯ ☐ ◯ ☐

Kaya has 50 cherries. She puts 10 cherries on each cake. How many cakes have cherries?

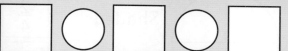

☐ ◯ ☐ ◯ ☐

Ellis has 7 vases and puts 10 flowers into each vase. How many flowers are there altogether?

☐ ◯ ☐ ◯ ☐

Caie has 8 pages in his sticker book. He puts 10 stickers on each page. How many stickers altogether?

☐ ◯ ☐ ◯ ☐

Poppy has 100 buttons. She needs 10 buttons to make a shirt. How many shirts can she make?

☐ ◯ ☐ ◯ ☐

Teacher's notes

Children read each word problem carefully, then write the multiplication or division calculation in the spaces provided.

41

Date: _____

Colouring fractions

Find $\frac{1}{2}$, $\frac{1}{4}$, $\frac{2}{4}$ and $\frac{3}{4}$ of a shape and write the matching fraction

You will need:
- coloured pencils
- ruler

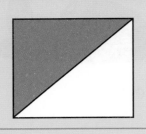 Shaded $\frac{1}{2}$

Not shaded $\frac{1}{2}$

Shaded $\frac{1}{4}$

Not shaded $\frac{3}{4}$

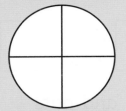 Shaded

Not shaded $\frac{1}{4}$

 Shaded $\frac{2}{4}$

Not shaded

Shaded $\frac{1}{4}$

Not shaded

Shaded

Not shaded $\frac{1}{4}$

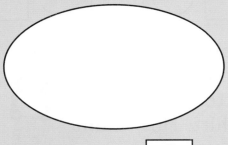 Shaded $\frac{2}{4}$

Not shaded

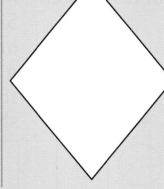 Shaded $\frac{3}{4}$

Not shaded

Teacher's notes

Children shade, or draw lines and shade each shape to match the fractions. Then they complete the missing fraction where needed.

ollecting quarters

se different combinations of one, two
nd three quarters to make whole squares

Date: _____

You will need:
- coloured pencils
- Resource 1:
  Quarters dice (or
  fractions dice)

Teacher's notes

Make up the quarters dice from Resource 1 (or use a fractions dice marked in the same way). With a partner, children take turns to roll the dice and colour in that amount of quarters in a single square of the grid. Rolls cannot be split, so if the player cannot colour that amount, they miss a turn. The winner is the first player to colour their whole grid.

Sweet share

Date: _____

Find half of an amount; find the whole amount when half is known

You will need:
- counters or cubes to use as sweets

$\frac{1}{2}$ of 6 = ☐

$\frac{1}{2}$ of 4 = ☐

$\frac{1}{2}$ of 10 = ☐

$\frac{1}{2}$ of 20 = ☐

$\frac{1}{2}$ of 14 = ☐

$\frac{1}{2}$ of 2 = ☐

$\frac{1}{2}$ of ☐ = 4

$\frac{1}{2}$ of ☐ = 9

$\frac{1}{2}$ of ☐ = 6

Teacher's notes

Children use counters or cubes to help them find half of the number given. For the last three questions, children need to give each character the correct number of counters and count or add them to find out which number was halved.

44

Date: _____

ounter quarters

nd one-quarter or three-quarters of an
mount; find the whole amount when
ne-quarter or three-quarters is known

You will need:
• counters or cubes

$\frac{1}{4}$ of 8 = ⬜ $\frac{1}{4}$ of 4 = ⬜ $\frac{1}{4}$ of 16 = ⬜

$\frac{3}{4}$ of 20 = ⬜ $\frac{1}{4}$ of 24 = ⬜ $\frac{3}{4}$ of 12 = ⬜

$\frac{1}{4}$ of ⬜ = 3 $\frac{1}{4}$ of ⬜ = 7 $\frac{3}{4}$ of ⬜ = 6

Teacher's notes

Children use counters or cubes to help them find one quarter or three quarters of the number given.
For the penultimate two questions, children need to give each character the correct number of
counters and count or add them to find out which number was quartered. The last question asks the
children to find the whole amount when they know three quarters.

Date: _____

Quarter past

Tell and write the time, quarter past

School starts at

_____

_____ .

School ends at quarter past 3.

Playtime is at quarter past 10.

Playtime finishes at half past 10.

Lunch starts at

_____

_____ .

Lunch finishes an hour later.

How many minutes are there in an hour? ☐

How many minutes are there in half an hour? ☐

How many minutes are there in a quarter of an hour? ☐

Teacher's notes

Children draw times on the clock faces to match the written time or they write the time shown by the clock face. Then they answer the questions about time.

Date: _____

Quarter to

Tell and write the time, quarter to

It's $\frac{1}{4}$ to 2.

It's _____.

It's _____.

It's quarter to
7 already!

There are [ ] minutes in $\frac{1}{4}$ of an hour.

There are [ ] minutes in $\frac{1}{2}$ an hour.

There are [ ] minutes in an hour.

There are [ ] minutes in $\frac{3}{4}$ of an hour.

Teacher's notes

Children draw times on the clock faces to match the written time or write the time shown by the clock face. Then they complete the sentences about time.

Date: _____

Past or to?

Tell and write the time to quarter past and quarter to the hour

Quarter past
$\frac{1}{4}$ past

Quarter to
$\frac{1}{4}$ to

1.

quarter past 11

2.

_____

3.

$\frac{1}{4}$ to 10

4.

_____

5.

$\frac{1}{4}$ past 1

6.

_____

7.

half an hour
after Clock 1

8.

half an hour
before Clock 3

9.

half an hour
after Clock 4

Teacher's notes

Children either draw the hands to match the written time or time interval, or write the time shown by the clock face in the space provided.

Date: _____

ow many minutes?

ell and write the time to 5 minutes

10 past 5

_____

_____

_____

20 past 11

25 past 1

_____

_____

5 past 3

Teacher's notes

Children draw times on the clock faces to match the written time or write the time shown by the clock face in the space provided.

Maths facts

Number and place value

Numbers 0–20 and 0–100

0 1 2 3 4 5 6 7 8 9 10 11 12 13 14 15 16 17 18 19 20

0 10 20 30 40 50 60 70 80 90 100

Place value

10s	1s
4	2

  42 = 40 + 2

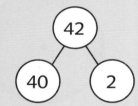

 42 = 30 + 12

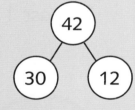

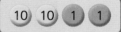 42 = 20 + 22

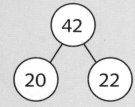

 42 = 10 + 32

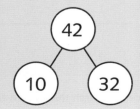

1–100 number square

1	2	3	4	5	6	7	8	9	10
11	12	13	14	15	16	17	18	19	20
21	22	23	24	25	26	27	28	29	30
31	32	33	34	35	36	37	38	39	40
41	42	43	44	45	46	47	48	49	50
51	52	53	54	55	56	57	58	59	60
61	62	63	64	65	66	67	68	69	70
71	72	73	74	75	76	77	78	79	80
81	82	83	84	85	86	87	88	89	90
91	92	93	94	95	96	97	98	99	100

Addition and subtraction

Addition and subtraction facts to 5, 10 and 20

+	0	1	2	3	4	5	6	7	8	9	10
0	0	1	2	3	4	5	6	7	8	9	10
1	1	2	3	4	5	6	7	8	9	10	11
2	2	3	4	5	6	7	8	9	10	11	12
3	3	4	5	6	7	8	9	10	11	12	13
4	4	5	6	7	8	9	10	11	12	13	14
5	5	6	7	8	9	10	11	12	13	14	15
6	6	7	8	9	10	11	12	13	14	15	16
7	7	8	9	10	11	12	13	14	15	16	17
8	8	9	10	11	12	13	14	15	16	17	18
9	9	10	11	12	13	14	15	16	17	18	19
10	10	11	12	13	14	15	16	17	18	19	20

+	11	12	13	14	15	16	17	18	19	20
0	11	12	13	14	15	16	17	18	19	20
1	12	13	14	15	16	17	18	19	20	
2	13	14	15	16	17	18	19	20		
3	14	15	16	17	18	19	20			
4	15	16	17	18	19	20				
5	16	17	18	19	20					
6	17	18	19	20						
7	18	19	20							
8	19	20								
9	20									

51

Half: $\frac{1}{2}$

 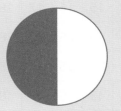  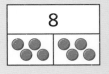

$\frac{1}{2}$ of 8 is 4

Quarter: $\frac{1}{4}$

 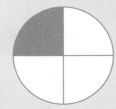  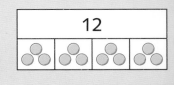

$\frac{1}{4}$ of 12 is 3

$\frac{3}{4}$ of 12 is 9

Multiplication and division

×	2	5	10
1	2	5	10
2	4	10	20
3	6	15	30
4	8	20	40
5	10	25	50
6	12	30	60
7	14	35	70
8	16	40	80
9	18	45	90
10	20	50	100
11	22	55	110
12	24	60	120

2 multiplication table

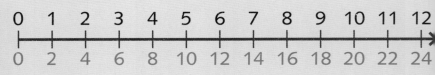

5 multiplication table

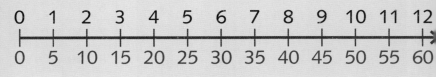

10 multiplication table

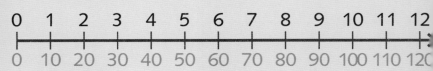

Measurement (time)

20 past 7 $\frac{1}{4}$ to 4

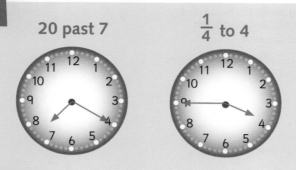

Position and direction

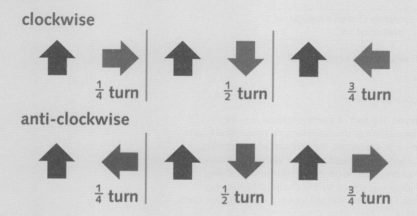

clockwise

$\frac{1}{4}$ turn $\frac{1}{2}$ turn $\frac{3}{4}$ turn

anti-clockwise

$\frac{1}{4}$ turn $\frac{1}{2}$ turn $\frac{3}{4}$ turn

Properties of shapes

2-D shapes

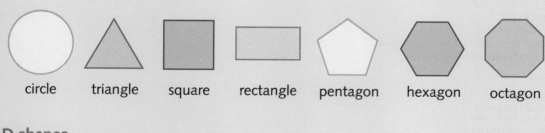

circle   triangle   square   rectangle   pentagon   hexagon   octagon

3-D shapes

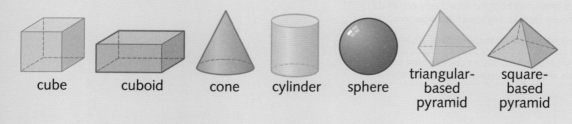

cube   cuboid   cone   cylinder   sphere   triangular-based pyramid   square-based pyramid

William Collins' dream of knowledge for all began with the publication of his first book in 1819.

A self-educated mill worker, he not only enriched millions of lives, but also founded a flourishing publishing house. Today, staying true to this spirit, Collins books are packed with inspiration, innovation and practical expertise.

They place you at the centre of a world of possibility and give you exactly what you need to explore it.

Collins. Freedom to teach.

Published by Collins

An imprint of HarperCollins*Publishers*
The News Building, 1 London Bridge Street, London,
SE1 9GF, UK

HarperCollins*Publishers*
Macken House, 39/40 Mayor Street Upper, Dublin 1,
D01 C9W8, Ireland

Browse the complete Collins catalogue at
collins.co.uk

© HarperCollins*Publishers* Limited 2023

10 9 8 7 6 5 4 3 2

ISBN 978-0-00-861331-0

All rights reserved. No part of this publication may be reproduced, stored in a retrieval system, or transmitted in any form by any means, electronic, mechanical, photocopying, recording or otherwise, without the prior written permission of the Publisher or a licence permitting restricted copying in the United Kingdom issued by the Copyright Licensing Agency Ltd, 5th Floor, Shackleton House, 4 Battle Bridge Lane, London SE1 2HX.

British Library Cataloguing-in-Publication Data

A catalogue record for this publication is available from the British Library.

Series editor: Peter Clarke
Cover design and artwork: Amparo Barrera
Internal design concept: Amparo Barrera
Designers: Steve Evans
Typesetter: David Jimenez
Illustrators: Helen Poole, Natalia Moore and Aptara
Printed in India by Multivista Global Pvt. Ltd.

MIX
Paper | Supporting
responsible forestry
FSC™ C007454

This book is produced from independently certified FSC™ paper to ensure responsible forest management.

For more information visit: harpercollins.co.uk/green

Busy Ant Maths 2nd edition components are compatible with the 1st edition of Busy Ant Maths.